The Purple Wave

Are you ready to vote?

Written by Ashraya Ananthanarayanan

Dedicated to:

First and foremost, my wonderful parents, without whom my journey would never have begun. My first steps, my first words, my first reading, my first writing, you have held my hand through it all. Thank you for making me all that I have become.

My friends and family, who have pushed me to be the very best version of myself every day. Your daily encouragement keeps me going and empowers me beyond words.

Finally, my terrific teachers, who have constantly illuminated the path of knowledge along my journey. "A teacher affects eternity—their influence never ends." As such, thank you so very much.

Note from the Author

Dear Reader,

I should begin with thanking you for taking the interest to read this publication. With all intents to do precisely that, I'd like to walk you through my motivations towards writing *The Purple Wave*.

As a graduate from a legal studies/political science field, I never truly was able to grapple with the concept of democracy that we see executed in our country on a daily basis. Oftentimes, I found myself in a position considering whether or not I truly believed in the concept of democracy that was instilled into the deep roots of our nation's government, and how it would affect our generations to come.

People often ask me the question, "What would you change if you could change one thing about the world?" I'm still not too convinced on my answer for a scale as grand as the whole world, but I have arrived at an answer for what I would change about the country that I am proud to call home: inclusivity. No spoilers, though, read through the entire work to learn what exactly that means.

What is a "Purple Wave", exactly? In a short answer, you. Each and every one of the readers of this book are the purple wave that I am encouraging the start of. I have spent all my years exploring the depths of red (Republican) and blue (Democratic) waves move across the sea of voters when election season rolls around, and I have quickly come to learn that it is quite an ineffective method to affect change on society to categorize oneself as *blue* or *red*. My call to action is simple: join forces for one cumulative cause—improving American government. Dear *reds* and *blues*, it is time for you to join and become *purple*, the color that shows the world that we are a country of thoughtful voters, engaged public, and motivated change makers.

My fellow students, my colleagues, friends, and family, thank you for taking the time to read on, and for your support on this marvelous journey of learning.

Warm Regards,

Ashraya Ananthanarayanan

Introduction

"Let us not seek the Republican answer or the Democratic answer, but the right answer. Let us not seek to fix the blame for the past. Let us accept our own responsibility for the future."

It was a beautiful evening at Loyola College on February 18, 1958 when John F. Kennedy spoke these words. His words are just as applicable in the present day, six decades later.

Little is it recognized that there is a necessary amount of change in the system that America currently relies on. Every American is born with the privileges and responsibilities that build the foundation of the nation. Being able to create an effective set of changes that propel the society, as a whole, in the direction best suited to serve generations to come is the end result that any successful social entity would want to associate itself with. While it is an essential and keystone portion of the framework of the nation, it is currently being disregarded, and left to the existing frameworks that are in place, if only to serve the country with simplicity and non-opinionated rights or authorities.

The year 2016 was inarguably amongst the most impressive for politics that the United States has seen in recent times. Each level of the election was intensely followed, polarized, and, essentially, sensationalized. Therefore, it is inevitable that conflict has arisen, as well. The campaigning season of 2016 was a reflection of who the American people are--a reflection that brought to light the necessity to reevaluate current political thought processes that are employed by American voters across all states and backgrounds.

Where our magnificent country thrives in the face of collaboration and an organizational framework that behooves that level of cooperation amongst all who have a stake in its success, it is currently in a predicament whereby there are questions of it retaining its pride and ability to stand as a superpower and dream nation. Initially fantasized as the land of opportunity and the new world, the lack of coordination between multiple portions of the country has left it in utter discord and a cry for help has risen from the ashes of the once truly great institution.

The beloved Constitution, upon which the American government has been built out, has been tossed and played catch with, and the cries of the words penned so carefully upon it have been drowned out by the ritualistic calls of the opposition between the two main parties dominating in the White House: the Democratic and Republican parties. While there are merits in the functioning of the system as is, seeing as it has created an entity that today still stands as a mark of greatness renowned, the world has changed notably in multifarious political manners, demanding a consequent and equivalent level of change to be put across the governmental framework of the current day.

The American public, the voters who prize their democracy, are being driven to have to question whether democracy is truly present, and whether it is profoundly given purpose through the actions of the citizenry. The Millennial generation, in collaboration with the upcoming members of Generation Z and generations beyond, is having to face the question of how they will repair their broken nation, and how they will diminish the cracks that have appeared in the mirror of the beautiful American reflection.

The pillar that makes our initiatives worthwhile and stable as a country is the promise that it will create a better tomorrow. How effective is the creation of a better tomorrow if those who will be living in that period are unsatisfied with the efforts that are being employed, though? What is the merit in including a copious amount of dedication to the creation of a brighter future when there are questions surrounding the effectiveness of the current practices in play that are being built upon further? Is it, indeed, sensible to build on a shaky foundation, only to anticipate failure that will have to be demolished and reconstructed? And, of course, who is capable of empowering such change?

Can the youth step up to the plate and swing confidently? If the current situation continues to persist, it seems highly unlikely. It has been said time and again that a country is only as great as its people. Therefore, the next generation of American youth must be groomed to greatness, as they are empowered with a government that supports their endeavors, and absolves differences between them. The United States of America must live up to the name "united", and this task is one that shall propose great levels of difficulty, as it requires an immense amount of dedication from one and all.

What is the solution?

It consists of several parts. The first step of analysis surrounds the candidacies that are present for governmental positions that hold the power to represent the people. The second is an analysis of how to allow for the eligibility criteria to be modified for a leader to be brought into governance. The last part, and the action that will redefine the shape of American politics to bring it to absolute greatness, will be that of incorporating the present generation into key positions that afford them the power to become decision makers involved in the very laws that govern their future.

With each of these components, time, dedication, and support are crucial. Are the American people willing to step up their game? Can we truly make the American nation we are proud to call home great?

Voices of Voters

The history of the American government is rich, indeed. But it is also a story that holds many controversies and secrets within its pages. Many, many years ago, there existed two main parties, which highly resemble the two main parties that we can see in the present day. In the past, the Anti-Federalists and Federalists existed to debate the framework upon which the United States of America was built. There were continuous debates surrounding the structure of power that should be delegated, the levels of power allocated to each appropriate governmental entity, and whether, in fact, power should be allocated centrally at all.

The Federalists believed in the existence of a strong central government, one which could hold the reigns and survive the chaos that was inevitable after the dramatic changes that had occurred at the time. Therefore, between the years 1796 and 1828, the two parties formed to hold opposite ends of the spectrum on this matter. In this time, the Constitution was developed, and the government was given a support structure to rely on. Essentially, the Federalists won their cause, but their party was left in shambles.

The opposing party, that which had referred to itself as the Anti-Federalists, became widely known as the Democratic-Republican party, one which believed in holding the Constitution above even the federal government, so that the centralized powers could be controlled. Over time, these systems have evolved into the existence of the parties that the country recognizes as the two independent parties of the Democrats and the Republicans. The split between the two parties into their respective separate entities occurred during the Era of Good Feelings after the 1824 presidential election, where the Democratic-Republican party was torn between two candidates: President John Quincy Adams and General Andrew Jackson.

Amongst the plethora of privileges given to an American citizen by the beloved Constitution, one of the key ones that gives every citizen a responsibility is the power to vote. Declaration of an entity as a democracy requires the ability to have voices heard through the form of a vote. But what is a vote?

In essence, a vote is a reflection of one's voice. Every American citizen is given the opportunity to present their voice and opinion in the form of their vote. Today, that vote has become insignificant and a demotivation, in fact, for many, in the contribution of the governmental actions of the States. For instance, in the 2016 presidential election, only 60.1 (sixty point one) percent of eligible voters turned out to actually present their vote. The more shocking fact, however, is that this was one of the highest numbers that has been seen in recent times for turnout for elections, both presidential and midterm[1]. Of course, this then begs the question--why?

Why would the American populace refrain from taking advantage of this wonderful privilege given in the form of the ability to vote? After all, the decisions made by the party who takes office will affect all citizens, not just the ones who decided to appear at the booths. Is it not crucial for every voter to be able to proudly assert their engagement with their nation, their opinions on their leaders, and their part in their futures?

In actuality, voters have little faith in their voices being heard, because they are unable to connect with the visions and messages of those standing to potentially take their seats in the White House and other governmental divisions. If a voter happens to find an independent party with whom they do indeed connect and see a positive spiral of future decisions for the country, they shirk their responsibility, because it is almost an indisputable fact that the candidate has no chance of a win amongst the larger names represented by the major parties in play.

Is a nation a true democracy if only sixty percent (and oftentimes less) of the citizenry actually has their voice represented in the election? Are the decisions that are made truly representative of the voices of all Americans? One study shows almost laughable answers to these questions. In 2018, American satisfaction with the way that the government is running daily functions touched an all time low at thirty eight percent[2]. Sixty two percent of people are not satisfied with the way that the government runs the country. This includes, indubitably, a majority of the forty percent (or more) of voters who did not turn out to the elections, and a decent portion of those who even did.

It does shed light on the voting process that, although the voter turnout was at an all time high, citizenry satisfaction is at an all time low. One facet of this leads to that of conspiracy theorists, and increases thought processes that may propagate discrepancies surrounding the reported votes that were recorded in favor of one party or another. The more important facet, one that does merit extensive understanding, though, is the discussion surrounding what a voter needs to see in the polls to actually make a sound voting decision. It follows logically to say that an unsatisfied voter is as good as a nonvoter, or an uninformed voter. When a member of the public approaches a booth to give their vote away to a candidate, they look for a level of trust that they can have in the party that they are voicing their support for. There is a certain level of liability that they impose on the party that they are awarding their vote to, such that the party is empowered to make decisions on the voter's behalf that support their viewpoints, the very ones that were expressed in their respective campaign. Theoretically, this should be the ideal voter: one who rewards a candidate with their support of that candidate's morals, ideas, and plans.

In today's voting "marketplace", votes are, for all intents and purposes, sold to propaganda and divisive politics. Rather than voting for an individual, citizens take to the stands to vote against another. The power in numbers is absolutely crushed and diminished in value, as a voter becomes nothing more than a means to achieve a trophy of a presidency, or other governmental position of power. This is the environment that the American population has given rise to. This is the reality has been brought to life through the buy in of the preached propaganda. The government is meant to be an entity that holds the country together, and makes sure day to day operations at all levels are seamless, or as close as they can be to that ideal, for the citizenry. Flawed political systems have allowed for corruptions and divisiveness to creep in, and these lurk among the shadows cast at voting booths, whispering sweet nothings to voters, who then become unsatisfied with the results that are presented after the voting.

In truth, a voter can only have the power to voice themselves when every candidate standing for elections has equal footing and prominence in the voting process. During campaigning season, a voter should not have to steer their thoughts towards the effectiveness of their vote, but rather the direction of their vote. The root of this issue is at the very core of elections, though, in the form of the ability for candidates representing multiple parties to have a decent chance at winning.

In a study conducted with a small sample of individuals at the midterm elections, about three hundred and forty voters scattered across various localities and demographic spans, there were some enlightening facts discovered about voter habits. The survey was short, succinct, and quite clear with there only being one question being posed to the various types of voters who were part of the collaborative study. "Who will you vote for today?"

It seems like a reasonable question, for which one would typically expect to receive reasonable answers. Furthermore, it stands to reason that a voter would come into an election with an intention to cast their vote for a particular individual. Strangely enough, though, in spite of the question being rather straightforward, the answers were relatively irrelevant.

"I'm voting Dem."

"I'm voting Republican."

"I'm voting red."

"I'm voting blue."

Without anticipation of such a response, those conducting the study were put on the spot to push the conversation a bit further. There was a clear requirement to assess the nature of the typical voter in more depth to fully understand how the voters arrived at their decisions, and why they automatically defaulted to answering with party names instead of the names of the individuals for whom they did intend to cast their vote.

Once again, the answers did little to shed light and instead cast overbearing confusion across the members of the study, because they were almost all identical, and predominantly all unwavering from their initial stage of being irrelevant answers. "Because I have always voted for that party", or various variations of this statement were those recorded by the conductors of the survey. It does strike as a feature of an extremely divided society when one is able to particularly section off the groups of voters into supporters of a party instead of supporters of a candidate.

In a rather rudimentary comparison, one New York based researcher wrote "How would you feel if your child ran for student body president as part of the 'Jock Party' and his or her contender was the 'Queen Bee' party of high school?" Strangely enough, the validity of this intriguing analogy is conspicuous. It facilitates a series of thoughts surrounding the question "why". Is there a particular motivation for voters in the present day to dissociate from the candidate and instead default to blindly seeing the mission statement of the party? Establishing a group that has prevalence in the political atmosphere is one thing. Creating a following that is deviated from the concept of voting fairly and is biased towards that party for the basis of that group's original vision is another. In a sense, voters are committing fraud if they are placing their opinions on the ballots presented to them solely on the basis of the party that the candidate they choose stands from.

It is time for the Millennial generation to wake up. A voter is given the privilege in this estimable nation to put forth their perspective, and make their choice of a leader count because they have a want to make their voice heard. In the present day, however, the voters are oblivious to their power, and they abuse the provision given through the Constitution for this rather impactful action that (incorrectly) supposedly has such a small impact. It appears the voters of today have forgotten the saying "Little drops of water make an ocean."

Statistically, one in every three voters who participated in the 2018 midterm elections did not know their candidates' names until they approached the voting booth, and seven in every eight Americans did not know what their candidate stood for[3]. The voters' eyes slid right past the names on the ballot to the color associated, whether that be blue or red, or the emblem representing that party. For a populace that boasts democracy, the American voters need to ask themselves, "Are we truly living in a democracy?"

Frankly speaking, the answer would be yes. Governmentally, American citizens enjoy the multitude of benefits associated with democracy each day. However, where the citizenry enjoys the benefits of the democracy that has been gifted, the responsibilities that come with it are disregarded, and America is fostering a society, an entire generation of individuals, to continue doing the same. When conducting a survey by asking one hundred post-secondary students from a political science field how many parties there are in the United States, more than sixty percent of them answered with the number two. Two political parties. In the eyes of the next generation of leaders, there are two political parties in the United States. In reality? Well, the real situation is that there are over twenty, with at least five widely acknowledged parties, amongst which the Republican and Democratic parties are only two. The Libertarian, Green, and Constitution parties are three other prevalent parties that are not even given complete recognition by all fifty states. Therefore, it is inevitable that the American citizenry would be oblivious to their existence.

The advocacy trying to be achieved is not to simply acknowledge the existence of other parties, though. That would not result in any improvement in the knowledge base of the voters of the United States. The action that is necessitated, rather, is to analyze how the predominance of two parties alone is impacting the voters of the present day. Voters are unknowing of who they are voting for, in all aspects. They hold no answers regarding what their candidate stands for, what qualifications their candidate possesses, and, in several cases, what their candidate's name is. The only image painted for an American voter is whether the candidate they are choosing is blue (Democratic) or red (Republican).

By definition, a voter should take into account three basic characteristics about their chosen candidate before placing their vote: the candidate's personal views, the candidate's background and qualifications, and the candidate's moral character. During a campaigning season, a voter should listen in keenly to the speeches given by their choices of candidates, and do their research to determine their affinity for that individual, and how well suited they believe that candidate would be the job.

For all intents and purposes, it is assumable that the presidency is a job--an occupation. It is hierarchically difficult to imagine the entirety of the citizenry being in a position of authority above this coveted title, but that is precisely what citizens are. A body of power that bestows the powers, title, duties, and responsibilities of government to the chosen leaders. Up until the point where a candidate takes office, the body of voters are essentially an employer to that candidate. When an employer receives several applications for a job opportunity, they would not dismiss a candidate because they do not hail from one of two major universities, for instance. They would look at the application in its entirety, and base their decision off of the credentials of each candidate, their previous show of experience and ability to do the job, their personality and fit for the culture, and, of course, their qualities of leadership exhibited through an interview.

When an employer of a company as small as a three member team does this extensive of a process to integrate a leader into their organization, does it not follow that a citizenry of 328 (three hundred and twenty eight) million should take a thousand times as much consideration for the choosing of a leader? The current campaigning system, combined with the empowerment of today's technology, gives a voter all of the power to make an informed decision about their vote, one that sees beyond party affinity or association. A candidate's background and qualifications are found through a simple Google or LinkedIn search. Of course, "qualifications" can be a rather broad term, as far as a position of power in a presidency form or other governmental form is concerned. To this means, consider the following: would a candidate with no experience in coding or software development, but ten years of experience in real estate advisory, be hired for the capacity of Technological Director at a multinational tech firm? The chances are rather slim, in fact, negligible.

The next facet of consideration is the personal views that a candidate holds. Observing these requires a bit more of dedicated research on the party in concern. Our process of elections has allocations for learning these factors about individuals, as well, though. By listening in to the speeches that are given by candidates, as well as looking through their social media exchanges, there is very little wiggle room for a candidate to misrepresent their views. Technology empowers us to be able to get in on the discussions surrounding the campaigns and campaigning processes of each candidate today, and voters can bounce opinions off of one another to be able to truly understand what a particular candidate may support or be against.

Unfortunately, the voters' knowledge today has been skewed to assume that a candidate's views are one and the same with the party's views. While a candidate may represent a particular party because their judgment most closely aligns with that of the party they are standing from, it is not a representative enough measure of their aptitude for leadership or their alignments in the political atmosphere to observe what their party supports. In fact, it is quite misleading to look at the perspectives of a party when choosing a candidate to support. There is little support for this point needed beyond the divisions of voters today. In the present day, approximately twenty five percent of voters consider themselves to be aligned with Republicans and the Republican party. Another thirty one percent of voters consider themselves to be Democratic, or align with the Democratic party. Over forty percent of voters consider themselves to be independent, or neither in support of the Democratic nor Republican parties[4].

These independent voters are the key to revolutionizing the way that leadership functions in the United States. Alone, this group of individuals can revamp the two party system that has left sixty two percent of Americans unsatisfied with the functions of the government on a day to day basis[5]. Although they consider themselves to be far and few between, these independent voters are, quite honestly, the most powerful group of voters in the country, as well as the most prevalent. Independent parties are paid no heed to for the sole reason that they have no visible support. The supporters who do come out to encourage these independent candidates are minimal, not because the candidates themselves have little support, but because the portion of this forty percent is unwilling or unaware that their vote will make a tremendous difference.

Apart from qualifications and personal views, a candidate's moral character is so absolutely pivotal as a matter of consideration when choosing a leader for the country. Evaluating the character of an individual is, in and of itself, a multifaceted topic.

If all three of these matters are taken into consideration when a voter is selecting the candidate they stand in support of, the next generation of leaders will be enriching, and far more impactful than administrations that have taken office without these matters being considered.

Focusing upon the first aspect of this matter, the candidate's personal views are crucial components to consider when having them be present as candidates to represent the people. However, in the present day, this is highly confused with the candidate's party's views. These are two very, very separate entities. The perspective that a candidate holds regards them as an individual, as a component of society that lives in the same environment that the voters do. The perspective of the candidate's party put this at a level above the viewership of the voters, where there is a bird's eye view of the occurrences that affect the voters on a day-to-day basis. While both are, indeed, crucial when considering voting, the first perspective a candidate must present to the voter is that of personal connection. Why can the candidate connect with the thoughts of the people? How well can the candidate represent the people they are striving to receive support from?

This is especially important at the levels of local and state elections. When there is an individual being chosen to represent a community, a close knit group of individuals, whether that be a locality, a county, or a state, this individual steps up as the sole contributor to showcase all of the ideas consolidated into one entity at a federal and national/international platform, as well. Therefore, it is integral to ensure that the individual is able to represent the citizenry appropriately. Candidates must provide answers on their perspectives on matters that echo deeply with the citizenry, and reasoning to support their judgment.

Communities shape and define the morals and values that they preach. A community should be in alignment with their elected leaders on a deep enough level to entrust that individual with the responsibility of being the spokesperson for a very large group of diversified, opinionated individuals. In order to successfully navigate the path of being a representative that will encourage the community to participate in political discussions and keep themselves abreast of current occurrences to make sure that they have an active attitude in their duties to the entity, the individual being put up to their respective position in Washington must be quite critically gauged during the campaigning period of their election season.

To recap, there are two steps to making sure that voters see the percentage of Americans who are satisfied with the government's doings proceed continuously upwards. To begin with, the one, foremost, crucial step is to encourage the public to be part of the decision making process. With nearly nine out of every ten American citizens having technological access and active smartphone usage today, it is uncanny to see such a low number in the capacity of those who choose to vote. It is pertinent that the responsibility of casting a vote is not shirked. At the same time, the citizenry must remain motivated in order to actually go forward towards making that move. To that means, there is a second requirement.

Opening up the ballots to incorporate several more candidates who are otherwise given little to no opportunity to even be considered for their respective positions will be a key move in bringing more voters to the table. It is a rather simple concept. The more options that are provided, the more positive attention that will be drawn from a group of individuals, motivating them to move forward with conducting an action, such as voting, or supporting a candidate. These independent parties, or otherwise declared parties that are separate from the two party system, overall, are doing more than their part in ensuring that the community is given the opportunity to hear from them. With no support from larger entities, though, there is no doubt that there will be a lack of recognition accorded to them, therefore driving less public association, and, in turn, a reduced voter turnout.

In the past, a plethora of reasons have been associated with the decreased voter turnout, or the lower number of Americans who vote as compared to the anticipated or goal number of individuals appearing to the booths. Amongst these, the most popularly presented theories include a lack of interest in candidates, an inability to cast votes electronically, an overall dissatisfaction with the government, etc. Two out of these three problems mentioned can absolutely begin to be addressed by incorporating more freedom for voters to make their choice between multiple parties. Giving the populace an opportunity to support the candidates who they believe truly represent them will overall create a much more positive wave of difference in the ways in which the public interacts with the government, and contributes back, engaging to create and facilitate the sorts of community collaboration that are being sought out through various initiatives put out by the White House.

Towards this means, there is no better place to start other than to have states begin to fully offer recognition to these parties, allowing more flexibility in creating additional entities that would like to stand for candidacy in any particular dimension. While there are currently 224 (two hundred and twenty four) state-level ballot-qualified political parties, 102 (one hundred and two) of these are actually made up of the Democratic and Republican parties. The Libertarian party receives qualification level representation from thirty seven states, while the Green party receives that level of recognition from twenty six states, and the Constitution party rounds up to a total of fourteen states. Disappointingly, then, it is shown that where these parties begin their approach to having support from the public, they are crushed because of not having the ability to even be represented on the ballots in an unfair majority of states that make up the United States of America.

Even so, the three minor political parties elaborated upon still only constitute a few of the dozens of minor political parties that do actually partake in political advocacy and running for leadership positions. The only way to move for states to qualify these parties, and in turn, all qualifiable candidates, is to encourage voters to get to their aid and support them, for instance by contributing to their required percentage of a winning vote. With over twenty candidates, it becomes much easier for the average voter to find a candidate who does speak to their ideals and the changes that they would like to see incorporated into the political framework of the country. It is said in several cultural contexts that there are representatives in multiple capacities to carry forth the messages that are preached, simply because it is not possible for each message to be individually delivered. In a similar capacity, every elected official acts as a mechanism for there to be acknowledgment and representation for entities that would not otherwise be able to have their voice heard.

The second part of change that needs to accomplished to see a happier overall public is to make it easier for candidates to be seen on a granular level for what they represent, rather than seeing a vaguer representation of what their party stands for. At the end of the day, a candidate represents a particular political party because their ideals more or less coincide with that of the party's, and their motivations to create change are primarily based on the mission of that party. That is, speaking truthfully ideally. In examples that have become vividly clearer over the past few decades, it is evident that this is a bit of flawed perception. While there is certainly an active movement and encouragement that candidates have to represent their parties ideologically in their political endeavors, it is far from the truth to believe that this occurs flawlessly, or even often. For instance, there have been leaders who have encouraged overall diversification in the country, bringing in skilled workers to boost the American economy, and then conducted actions such as restricting visa applications. There are yet other leaders who insist that they are strongly held against oppression of any sort, but in action promote divisive politics, encouraging communities to clash with one another.

Speaking more specifically to issues that tend to drive major differences between parties, there are candidates who stand with the perception of supporting anti-abortion movements, boasting and preaching the messages that come along with that movement, but rather have been the conductors of such actions themselves, on multiple occasions, as a mark of a poor judgment of words and actions. Leaders commonly are judged by an old saying, "walk the talk". As is true of any relationship, it is crucial to see a leader who is able to be true to his or her people by speaking their intentions loud and clear, and acting on them to promote unity within a country.

In any case, divisive politics is not only intimidating, but insidious in nature. The passive aggressive nature of it promotes communities to be riled up against one another, encourages leaders themselves to make bold, yet impractical and uneducated statements driving further wedges between the communities, and overall creating a strong voter base, but a very broken public to lead. This individual nature is not one that is inherently political, but rather one that is inherently personal, visible on many levels of social interaction that are easily enraptured through the beauty of social media that is present as a device for delving into an individual's personality today.

As an unfortunate parallel, individuals tend to lean towards leaders who do, indeed, choose to lead them upon this path of division, because they are radically aligned with only one side of what the leader presents, and blindsided with regards to seeing the consequences upon the community. In recent times, there have been innumerable instances of this being seen rather widely, especially with violent forms of demonstration and protest becoming the norm to try to balance out the nature of commotion that this type of politics has inherently created. The United States of

America gained the privilege of being referred to as the "melting pot" as the cultural pluralism spread in the 1940s. In the eighty years following that period, the rifts that have been created and followed through have diminished the value that the superpower nation once did truly hold within its clutches. "Our people are our power." Politicians often use this statement loosely, as it seems, when they are not groomed and are unprepared to be in political fields, especially as they refer to the American public, a highly diversified entity.

Today, it is nearly impossible to hide traits of inbuilt racism, discrimination, or bias of any sort when appearing for candidacy for an elected position. The individual standing is required to present themselves at multiple public events, some of which are scripted prior, but many of which require media presence that is conducted without any sort of prior preparation. Furthermore, candidates post nearly daily updates to their social media accounts, and have long term social media presences developed far before their candidacy that are available for viewing and for analysis. Conducting a heavy investigation on each individual that is brought into consideration for running for a political capacity is a failsafe, one meant to encourage voters to be more engaged with their vote, and treating it as an investment, rather than a one time activity. In truth, that is what it is. It is an investment that will last the entire term of that individual's presence in their capacity. Depending on the vote, that could be a two year, four year, eight year, or lifelong investment on each voter's part. Imagine investing in a property without a title check, without a home inspection, and without a walkthrough—just a direct purchase. Surely, even reading that statement would incite shaking heads, thinking that goes along the lines of "not smart".

Just as such, when each voter begins to understand that the value of their opinion and that single check mark is as much as a precious investment would be, there will be visible change in overall voting behavior. Media sensationalism is entertaining, but it is not a favorable trait in a candidate who intends to be a diplomatic leader in the

capacity to represent nationally, or even internationally.
Similarly, having a poor background in having well
founded political opinions, or being notorious for
promoting false political matters, is a basis that voters
should give heavy consideration to prior to assigning their
vote randomly. The decision made in those few seconds at
the booth will impact years of lifestyle, and the laws
created in that time will impact generations to come, likely.

All factors being taken into consideration, it is without
question that candidates are put to a grueling level of
testing during their period of standing for candidacy, and
beyond. Twitter has become a popularly recognized way of
sharing political opinions for most citizens and
representatives in the current day. Perhaps for the sake of
its simplicity, perhaps for the sake of its wide usage, the
platform has become an obvious way to be able to assess
the qualities in an individual as compared to the
presentation they give in their campaigning season.
Potential candidates can be assessed against their political
statements made in the past quite easily. If a candidate

speaks to encouraging diversity and community diversification overall, but posts or likes demeaning media on their social media platforms against specific communities, there is an evident discrepancy between their words and actions.

Similarly, more concrete aspects to rely on are presentable through actions as simple as a Google search. Simply taking the time to do a search on an individual will generate an immense amount of material that is rich with information surrounding that individual's history and alignment with their supposed political goals. In today's level of media coverage, every piece of newsworthy info will forever be available through the mechanism of the internet, and finding the sources of the information is quite easy. Once a voter has established reliable resources to go to and conduct their assessment of a candidate, their next step should be to put their gathered information in a side by side comparison to the presented information through that candidate's campaign. In and of itself, this process will be an apparent way of being able to create an accurate judgment of how to support an individual, as opposed to a party. Unfortunate as it is, the positions of office are treated as paid seats instead of meritoriously earned ones in the present day. These lesser candidates attempt to exploit the system by relying on an established voter segment for the party that they stand from, as opposed to meritoriously earning their place by gathering the supporters who they do, indeed, truly have for themselves.

To more clearly picture the level of support one truly has for a candidate versus a party, try the following: mentally swap out the candidate standing from the party in the primary support category with a candidate from another category, and reassess the level of support given to that candidate. If that level of support is any less, objectively or subjectively, the voter is still building opinions based on a party instead of an individual. It has been an ingrained, embedded habit over two hundred years of practice into various generations, thus making it inevitably a tough process to break away from. That being said, the rewards at the end of the process are indubitably immense, as they foster an ability to create a well founded basis for putting forward a vote.

Another aspect that several Americans struggle with when contemplating whether or not to support an independent party is how effective their vote will be. Oftentimes, a voter will be under the impression that their vote needs to "count", which is another way of saying that they intend to support the winning party, regardless of the impact that the party may have after taking their positions in Washington. In itself, this logic is flawed. If there were twenty million voters who believed that, individually, their votes would be insignificant if assigned to independent parties, that group could create waves of change, and drastically alter the polls. This is a rather intimidating move to make, especially when social pressures are such impactful decision making factors for these decisions. In a staggeringly large number of communities, there is either acceptance or nonacceptance based on the political stance of an individual, and how that individual chooses to vote when the time does come. This can often sway the manners of thinking that one possesses, tightening the grip on their insecurities and forcing their hand to put forth a vote that they do not wholeheartedly support. In turn, when the polls are released for how many individuals in the American public are truly satisfied with the conductions of the government, the numbers are drastically low.

Making every voter feel as though their true opinion matters is a task that is to be taken on by communities, as well. Demographically, some communities lend themselves to either support the Democratic or Republican parties because of their lifestyles and other differentiating factors, but they are far more split within their regions than the overall presiding political party. To accurately judge the political lean of a group of people, statistics must be interpreted on a much more granular level, associating individuals with the characteristics that embody particular parties instead of the names of the parties themselves. The results would be rather shocking for those who have been introduced to merely these two options: blue or red.

Having the choice between multiple candidates is a freedom that the American public is free to exercise—but are not plentifully or predominantly aware of yet, because of the lack of representation of the groups that could be their alternative options. While the essential political concepts being debated upon to create differentiation between the parties remain, at their core, the same, the various combination of missions and values allows for a more overall diversified set of candidates to choose from for the American people. In a study conducted in 2017, several voters (about 38 percent) stated that they would have preferred to have voted for an independent candidate if they had the opportunity to, or if that candidate had an equally promising support system across the nation. It is disappointing that the country, at large, fails these candidates who would otherwise stand as glorious representations of the idealism that American culture embodies in stating that various blends of people create the perfect medley in society[6].

Taking the discussion further away from ideals and morals, though, and into the concepts of political debate instead, these parties are all built upon the same framework. Although the issues that each party tackles, along with the respective rights and laws in place for those, are essentially the same, the manners in which they are approached vary significantly between each party. Take, for example, the perspectives of the widely known Libertarian party. Highly advocated as one of the most prevalent minor parties, the Libertarian party holds views that are predominantly centered around the concepts of political autonomy and independence. They hold beliefs that strongly coincide with personal choice, and put an emphasis on "every situation is different" when passing overall measures for prospective changes in the way in which the government views particularly striking issues. While they do believe heavily in following traditional systems that fundamentally create political and economic bases as they are known, there is an inherently created need to exercise caution when according power to any central or decentral authority, as per their organizational values.

For a majority of Americans who do not hold particularly strong views that would fall left or right, candidates of this party may actually strike them as much more appropriate choices than others who hold more radical or emphasized views. However, there is no doubt that the majority of two particularly new voting segments to the addition, Millennials and Generation Z, would vote in the favor of these types of parties heavily. Over and above 65 percent of individuals who fall into one of these two generational groups believes that self autonomy and self governance is by and far the best way to be able to successfully create a governmental framework that does work for all[7]. In fact, this concept has spread so far that up and coming startup firms are even practicing decentralization of power from the very start of their enterprise, ensuring that their methods are not only more effective than traditional methods, but also arriving at a higher employee happiness ratio, and thus increasing overall productivity within the organization.

The concepts that individuals believe in do often translate between the corporate workspace and the social atmosphere that they encourage to develop in the context of an entire social framework. The creation of a society as a tiered, multi-level entity that follows a set of either particularly conservative or particularly liberal workflows is nearly obsolete in this day and age, with the majority of individuals who follow such a method for creation of an entity being unaware of how to incorporate present day methods successfully, and often deferring to other successful enterprises that do incorporate the modernization tactics that embody the political atmosphere, as well. The coincident between society, workspaces, and politics has long been known to be an oddly engineered one. There are several parallels to be drawn, many tangents to be observed, and quite a few conflicts that arise between all three segments that make up the entirety of human interactivity.

Specifically in the United States of America, it has been long seen that the political atmosphere is highly emphasized by the ways in which people see their environment evolve on a social and corporate level daily. The needs and wants of the public are respectively incorporated as per the evolution of society as time progresses, and where change is heavily anticipated and welcomed in some arenas, other arenas are full of untapped potential because they simply enter into a field that has been unexplored by the present ideologies that dominate the political field in Washington, therefore influencing the rest of the nation. It is time for the change to be brought for there to be enlightenment for each individual who contributes to the society, whether it be socially, politically, or otherwise. Change is inevitable, and quite beautiful when incorporated well. The change that is needed in the system is two part. Firstly, there is an absolute need for the voter-ship that actually partakes in casting their ballots to increase. This is facilitated by the second part of the needs of the new government, which would be to allow for the minor parties to stand as components or groups that contribute heavily towards the decisions that are made regarding who wins the elected position of office at any level, particularly including the House of Representatives, the Senate, and the presidency.

The only mechanism or vehicle of change is often the youth. These members of society hold the power to embody the change that they wish to see executed in their ideal world, and they have the privilege of being part of a community that is not only well empowered, but well connected and therefore able to facilitate change from the ease of their device. In this day and age, creating a petition and encouraging others to support it and sign it is as simple as creating a Facebook account or ordering a pizza, and having one's voice heard is often not an issue that deserves much complaint.

Nonetheless, there are changes that even the youth must push for at a deeper level than prior generations have been able to. The only way to bring true advocacy and change to a governmental platform is to begin to facilitate that change on a smaller level and draw attention to it in a sensational way. This technique is by and far the most effective marketing strategy for any entity, whether it be individual, product, or concept, but it will serve just as well in providing information to individuals who do, indeed, need it about the existence of these parties, and what level of support they need to truly become the change makers that they envision, as well. The chance to be seen is not one that is independently driven nor achieved. In order for a group to truly achieve that level of success, they require the aid of the most powerful campaigning tool available today: social media and influencer power.

The majority of the public gets their advocacy and inspirational sets of information from social media influencers in the present day. From looks to books to cooks, every factor that would affect daily life is harbored by several coveted influencers, who are able to create a following that is strong enough to convey meaningful messages if empowered in the right way. The most effective strategy to convey the existence of these additional parties and to push for their recognition and choosing is to encourage them to be "adopted" by social media influencers who do truly believe that their messages echo with that party. It is quite near impossible to find a singular party that does embody all of the ideals that one believes in, and that is what has motivated the majority of these influencers to steer clear of political engagement. But the interconnectivity between politics and society is strong enough that it is highly unlikely that any individual who considers themselves an influencer has been uncommunicative of political thought processes through their work or through their postings. Joining the movement for change in the candidacy system is not just a political statement that encourages equality, it is an opportunity to open up the platform of politics to several others who may otherwise have their voices drowned out in the present day commotion that takes place at Washington.

Allowing for there to be a larger diversity of parties in political representation decreases the pressure applied from a party to conform to a particular decision despite being personally diversified from the opinions being brought out in that decision making process. Indeed, this is the difficulty that a large sector of politicians who are in the responsibility of representing the public are facing today. The dilemma that they are constantly battling is whether to support the majority in their party who may vote strongly in one direction, or to vote their true opinion, which may vary greatly. This question has within it another inherent capability. It has the ability to create and embody an opportunity for more talented politicians to stand through ways in which they neither compromise the personal integrity of their moral compass for the sake of party politics, nor mislead the public by creating a rift between the perceived and the apparent.

Opening up the arena for individuals to perform their political duties at a level that is more honest to their true self identity will, in fact, create a far more effective overall government. Part of the reason that the American satisfaction levels are quite so low is because representatives themselves have a happiness index of less than 45 percent on average, essentially meaning that they believe personally in less than half of the decisions that they make on a daily basis. There are individuals with various sets of values throughout the world, some of whom inevitably do coincide very specifically with the belief systems propagated by the Democrats or the Republicans. In this case, advocacy is not being raised to overshadow those perspectives or the individuals who do present from that side of the argument, but rather to allow for the platform to expand and grow into newer horizons that incorporate a more diversified set of individuals, therefore resulting in richer political discussion, as well.

The practice of incorporating individuals into politics who hold different views from those who are either Democratic or Republican is a time consuming process. No doubt that the reception of these additional parties will continue to be as tough as it has been for the past century, at the very least. There is little to no question that there is room for improvement, but it is not a concept that will be welcomed with open arms, especially considering the very typically observed attitude towards government that "If it ain't broken, don't fix it." This concept serves as a root cause issue for the predominant set of ones that plague the majority of the Democratic and Republican leadership in current play. With the integration of those who hold unexplored opinions on the matters that are focal points of discussion, the attention towards various perspectives will no doubt be divided, and enriching. With the perfect mix between these two highly effective and driven qualities of establishing a governmental predominance, there will be everlasting positive change spirals that can begin to ripple through the system.

Redefining a Leader

Most American citizens grow excited as they approach their sixteenth birthday, because, in most states, they become eligible to apply for a driver's license. At their eighteenth birthday, they become eligible for a large number of other responsibilities, including:

- **The ability to vote.** At eighteen years old, a citizen is considered matured enough to make a decision about who the leadership in the country should be.
- **The ability to sign contracts.** Legal liability comes naturally with age, and the age of eighteen becomes the apparent point at which an individual is qualified to have that liability fall upon them.
- **The ability to own property.** As of the age of eighteen, individuals are able to become homeowners, completely furnished with the responsibility of home care, tax liability, mortgage premiums, etc.
- **The ability to pay taxes.** Since they become officially capable of working full-time, any individual at eighteen becomes responsible to pay and file their taxes as per governmental deadlines. In fact, those who begin work

before that age (since work permits are handed out for part-time work at the age of fourteen in many states) hold that liability on their paycheck far before they even reach eighteen.

- **The ability to own certain types of firearms.** While there are hot debates surrounding the ability to own firearms at any point, the current age requirement for owning some types of firearms (including shotguns and rifles) is eighteen in several states.

- **The ability to be tried in court as full adults.** As they reach the age of eighteen, individuals have the additional pleasant responsibility of being able to be tried in court as adults.

The list is endless, including the right to have an abortion, have a child, get married, get divorced, play the lottery, collect inheritance, open a bank account, buy cigarettes, etc.

As extensive as the set of rights accorded to eighteen year olds is in the United States of America, there is one crucial right that they are denied: the ability to run for office, in virtually any state or federal capacity.

"It's time to fundamentally change the way that we do business in Washington. To help build a new foundation for the 21st century, we need to reform our government so that it is more efficient, more transparent, and more creative. That will demand new thinking and a new sense of responsibility for every dollar that is spent."

Spoken by former President Barack Obama, these words serve as inspiration for change in many capacities. He emphasizes one word continuously in this statement, though: new. A *new* foundation. A *new* thinking. A *new* sense of responsibility.

"This world demands the qualities of youth: not a time of life but a state of mind, a temper of the will, a quality of imagination, a predominance of courage over timidity, of the appetite for adventure over the love of ease."

This time spoken by Robert Kennedy, another prominent political figure in Washington, the message begins to sink in. Several campaigns promoted through political endeavors cling to the support of the hope that "Our youth is our future." This, then, begs the question, should the youth who are meant to shape tomorrow not have a role in determining what that tomorrow looks like? The world is in dire need of a youthful perspective in matters related to collaborative leadership. It is an objective truth that the future of the American society is to be the most impactful upon the youth in the country, as they develop into the next generation of leaders. Therefore, it is integral to have their representation in positions where they can be heard, where their perspectives on global matters can be taken into account.

The average age of Members of the House at the beginning of the 116th Congress was 57.6 years; of Senators, 62.9 years. In contrast, the average age of acquiring politically fluency in the Millennial generation was 15 years; of Generation Z, 12 years[8].

These startling statistics of the present day owe to us the responsibility to look upon our actionability and see whether the youth is truly represented in the leadership that they are impacted by. A mere six percent of present day congressional members are under the age of thirty-five, and even amongst these, the youngest is of twenty-nine years.

The generation that is being groomed represents all but zero percent of the leadership in place.

It is cited by multiple sources that, between the ages of eighteen and twenty-five, nearly ninety-six percent of individuals hold employment, and nearly all of those individuals are involved in advocacy and change processes in corporate environments[9]. The question, then, remains to be why these individuals are not given the ability to stand for their own voices abreast the esteemed politicians of the nation.

Between exposure to political processes at national and international levels with activities such as Model United Nations, Junior State of America, student government, and student political clubs, as well as a rich technological empowerment that includes students of all ages in the current events around them, the upcoming generation is more prepared than ever before to be able to take charge in decision making at Washington. Every generation comes with the startling exponential growth of a knowledge base at an early age, and the current generation of business leaders and social leaders, the Millennials and Generation Z, are able to confidently step up to be the face of several facets of life. Accordingly, the political environment should fair well with their presence, as well. After all, there is quite nearly no one as well equipped to understand this generation's needs, wants, and expectations as spokespeople for their entity, themselves. The American government is full of wonderful leaders who bring to the table years of experience, insights, and wisdom, but lack the perspective, creativity, and inclusivity that upcoming generations have.

As far as political correctness goes, it is unseemly to suggest that age has an impact on perspectives, socially and morally speaking. It is, of course, widely foolish to make an assumption or generalization about the entirety of any generation based on a sample of that group. This stands true across platforms and entities. Regardless, the current world demands certain mental assets when determining policies and leadership. One of the easiest ways to understand the interpretation of this statement is through the lens of the most widely discussed issue in the present day: racism.

Over ninety percent of Generation Z supports the Black Lives Matter movement, and promote diversity and inclusivity at new levels within their organizations, whether they be existing teams in multinational corporations, or smaller teams at startups[11]. Similarly, there is support for LGBTQI+ individuals amongst over seventy percent of Americans between the ages of eighteen and twenty-five[12]. As a contrast, over forty percent of Americans between the ages of fifty-five and seventy-five believe that the Black Lives Matter movement does *not* need support, and should *not* be encouraged[13]. Furthermore, less than thirty percent of Baby Boomers and Generation X feel as though gay marriage should be legalized and supported[14].

Generation gaps exist—this is a psychologically proven concept. However, the prejudices that have been incorporated into former generations have seeded deeply enough that it is impossible to not have their influence on decisions made regarding policy and lawmaking in the United States. Although inadvertently, current lawmakers are infusing the governmental and legal structure of the country with bias, discrimination, and division. Furthermore, the very laws that are being made and passed, which are influenced by these biases, are rather brashly opposite to what the generation affected by those laws is seeking. Millennials and Generation Z predominantly envision a united country, one where all are included, and all feel as such.

Since the youth of the country have grown with inclusivity embedded into their daily environments, it is unnatural to them to promote anything contrary. As lawmakers, they will create a far more successful America, where social division is less, compassion is more, and good citizenship is a natural tendency, as opposed to a forcibly imposed necessity.

Furthermore, the youth can speak most fluently to the issues that affect them in the present day. With a growing number of students involved in political science, either academically or as an extra curricular, the future generations are becoming increasingly aware of how to battle the matters that befall ill to their communities. To understand at a greater depth what the effectuality of different generations is on growing pains in the current state of events of the country, several issues can be discussed.

Perhaps the most widely discussed issue that is of major concern in the present day is racism. To that means, the review above regarding the Black Lives Matter movement already presents a resounding impact. Furthermore, one can look at the ways in which the youth has been influenced by looking at diversity metrics in corporate organizations led by younger leaders.

Historically, companies that were started prior to 2005 are, in the present day, still falling short of being able to abundantly diversify their workforce, with the average being 28% diversification of race representation across the top two tiers of corporate entities[15]. In essence, this translates to having approximately four in every five positions monopolized by a singular race or ethnicity, thus providing an unnecessarily bleak perspective on corporate dynamics and their relativity to how the thought processes of those in the leadership capacities to make the call for diversification are presented.

On the other hand, startups and established firms created after 2005, those founded by recent graduates and those between eighteen and twenty-five years of age, have diversification percentages above 74%[16]. In broader terms, this represents that three out of every four members of a leadership team at one of these organizations are from different ethnic or racial backgrounds. Of course, speaking purely professionally, this serves as a means to assess how the corporate climate has evolved with time. In the present day, there would be significant bias in this position if one were to fail to acknowledge the recent increase of diversification programs that have been started by corporates of all types.

But at their core, at their creation, these ideals have separated the generations because of the ways in which social perspectives have influenced their decisions in future endeavors, as well. For an analogy, consider the following.

If Person A saw a practice of bias against cheese throughout childhood, although unspoken, and saw the discrimination practiced well into adulthood, the likelihood of Person A exhibiting that bias is arguably nothing short of one hundred percent. Now, if Person B was introduced to the existing conditions that Person A saw, but was brought up in an environment that suggested no discrimination against cheese themselves, they would more or less indubitably perceive cheese with a kinder eye. Furthering this concept, then, if Person A were to interact with Person B and Person B's society at length, it is likely that Person A's bias would decrease.

This is what the American citizenry see happening in the present day. Unfortunately, the consequences are much steeper when one is to deal with fellow community members in this fashion. The severity of those consequences increases a hundredfold when the decisions of this now softened, but at the core biased Person A makes the decisions that affect a community that is comprised of all types of people. Without the strong influence of Person B, it is unlikely that the leadership would succeed in creating effective, positive change.

Another matter that is seen prevalently and is heavily discussed in the present day is gender inequality. With the increasing number of individuals who are able to create and shape their identity as who they want, different positions have weighed in on the matter of the independence allotted to individuals to experience their lives and make those decisions for themselves as they seek to. While the politics surrounding this matter are diverse and both justified and not, acceptance of all types of individuals into a community is absolutely necessary to create harmony that several politicians boast about being able to create. Differences in opinion surrounding the abilities and validities of individuals discovering themselves are irrelevant, though, to the larger context of looking at how the divisive nature of separative politics is influencing decision making at governmental levels. Amongst the Millennial generation and Gen Z, there is an acceptance of over seventy percent for same-sex marriage. In generations prior, such as Baby Boomers, the acceptance was below forty percent. How does that affect political decisions?

It took over fifty years and thousands of riots (for example, the Stonewall Riots), mostly spearheaded by youth representatives, to allow for the simplest right: the choice to represent oneself as the gender that they identify as on documentation. The choice to marry the person of their choice is still under debate in many regions, and this, in turn, affects the fear factor that individuals have in being able to even openly express their identities to individuals. It affects the daily life of over twenty two million people—twenty two million of whom are fellow Americans, twenty two million of whom the country considers citizenry.

At the root of all of these issues, the environment that the newer generations have been brought up in is the key factor that sets them apart. Each generation promotes more and more inclusivity, and as a result, every following generation gets to experience a country that is filled with even more acceptance. Generation Z has been exposed to a country that is truly a melting pot, with nearly forty percent of the population being made of varying ethnic backgrounds and races, while the generations before lived in an environment that only had a maximum of fifteen percent of representation for other races, the majority of whom were still operating as subordinates to other ranks in society[17]. It is beautiful that the world the newer generation has the opportunity to live in is brighter in these ways and more. It is a blessing, but also a responsibility that these upcoming generations, therefore, hold to only further the efforts that have been in play by stepping up to leadership roles.

With a strong background now of why change is needed, the next suitable question is how change can be incorporated. Put simply, the current bodies of government that make lawmaking decisions on a daily basis need to incorporate youth representatives. Experience is invaluable, and cannot be replaced, nor recreated. It is said that there is no substitute for time on the job, and there are several merits to that statement. However, social dynamics and politics are matters of knowledge and experience as much as they are of psychology and empathy. This latter term, the ability to relate, is just as invaluable as experience, education, and every other credential that stands to represent the members of government who hold the estimable position of responsibility towards citizenry today.

Without a doubt, younger representatives will benefit from having a guiding hand in the form of several experienced colleagues beside them. In this way, though, at least the ideas and perspectives of the generation being governed can nudge their way into the congressional bodies for consideration. Overall, the implementation of this concept into the larger governmental framework that is in use today would be a marvelous effort that would serve as a highlight for the administration promoting it, entirely. To begin, it is essential to understand what avenues the youth, those under twenty-five, currently have available in the form of the wealth of resources for their use to get their opinions into the White House. While more obvious routes, such as joining a campaigning team or getting selected as a White House intern exist, larger numbers of students may only have the ability to make their presence known through the use of clubs, petitions, etc.

According to the United States' government, one of the best points of contact for the leaders in the making is to create a petition using the governmentally supplied platform "We the People". As opposed to reaching out individually to multiple senators or congress-people, "We the People" allows for petitions to be created that can then garner support from family members, community members, and others using the provided link. Petitions that reach the minimum required one hundred thousand signatures within thirty days will then be given an official response from the White House within sixty days.

Although a brilliant solution to being able to provide the opportunity for a multitude of issues to be arisen, this method proves particularly ineffective, as over forty percent of petitions that even did meet the specified requirements of one hundred thousand supporters within thirty days were given a nominal response with no point of following or guaranteed actionability. In addition, this method of use for contacting and communicating with the White House serves primarily as a way to comment on new social issues, and a proposal of replacing ineffectual methodologies in current play, as opposed to providing a platform to debate the merits of new policy prior to it being put into effect, and allowing for equal standing, commutative conversation. For all intents and purposes, the platform serves as a polite gesture that is akin to what corporates generally present as a "comments, concerns, and suggestions" box to their clientele.

Another method that is currently in existence for youth representatives of their communities to create waves of change is to approach each senator or governor in their respective localities through email or contact forms that are provided on their websites, or by posting a piece of mail to their office. Unfortunately, this method proves to be even more ineffectual than "We the People", as it stands to reason that several of the presented cases are lost amongst the whirlwind of communication that no doubt is received by an unused mailbox, either electronically or physically.

To further prove the point, if statistics and factoids do not serve as enough basis for reconsideration, simple logic may do the trick. The public manages to create waves of change when, and only when, the matter is sensationalized by the media. This then requires there to be a set of current events that are devastating enough to create outbursts of rage or protest amongst the communities of the United States, thus enabling the change makers to influence the discussions in the White House. Quite obviously, this is an utterly disgraceful and insanely disgusting way to have to create and empower the change that is sought to be seen in society or in government. Raising one's voice should not and is not the answer to creating change that our forefathers envisioned.

If one were to consider the matters that do not create social sensationalization, as well, such as climate change, international politics, and energy law, there is no way in which these young minds could contribute effectively. Continuing on this thought process, then, it stands to reason that the most amicable solution to allow for diversified inclusion between experienced and innovative minds is to include youth representatives within the conversations that take place surrounding any and all lawmaking and governing decisions. The rights provided to citizens through the very concept of democracy are in violation if any one member of that democracy is unable to be participative in reaping the benefits of it. In this scenario, it is not one, but over one hundred and twenty seven million who are being silenced in the name of lack of experience.

Including youth representatives into government is not a process that requires extensive analysis or forethought, because it does not include a capacity for replacement of current bodies, or changes in the legal processes that take place. Bodies of youth representatives should be subject to the same requirements as any other representative, including the need to be voted in during midterm elections, the ability to fund their own campaign and create a following that supports them, participate in the required debates and such to create awareness of their perspectives on different policy matters, and, of course, maintain their responsibility towards their judicial confidentiality and position. In order to deflect from delinquency being considered as an issue, there should be requirements of the completion of a high school diploma or equivalent qualification, as well, so as to ensure that the participants are not hindering their educational endeavors as legally mandated. Furthermore, these youth candidates should be subject to the same level of aforementioned rigorous testing that determines their level of knowledge of the Constitution, their region's laws and regulations, as well as their leadership capability. These critical components serve as additives to what the founders of the nation had envisioned to be able to foster a great America, indeed, one that surpassed the expectations of all that engaged with it, either through trade, or vocation, or residence.

The next question that would undoubtedly arise when discussing incorporating youth members into congressional divisions is, "How far should it go?" Which level of leadership is adequate to have the voices of the youth included in discussing the matters that surround their generations' perspectives? Is it adequate to have the powers that are accorded to the members of the House of Representatives and Senate, or should there be higher levels of representation, up and through the level of a presidency?

The majority of political decisions made in the present day fall under the scrutiny of the House and Senate prior to even being applicable to pass as laws or governance in the United States. As a result, to begin with, the level of inclusivity that should be sought out is an inclusion of youth into these two governing bodies. Above and beyond this measure, going into positions such as the presidency will take time to initially assess the effectuality of these new positions, as well as a consideration of how the requirements for the presidency itself adapts, as well. Every member of the government shoulders an incredible responsibility, and would do well to remember that.

The American government has an inbuilt capacity to incorporate more representatives, financially, as well. Between the founding of the country and the present day, several adjustments have been made to the original manner of division of monetary incentives for governmental representatives. Speaking on a historical basis, this originally commenced with a term of no payment for those who served in congressional divisions, or any facet of government, for that matter. The primary reasoning behind this was that those who served in government were generally very well to do, and that the incentive for being in government was for social service and esteem, as opposed to monetary sides of the coin.

As times changed, every industry adapted, and society evolved, this thought process was revisited, as well, and changed with the additive of a nominal six dollar payment for each day that congressmen served at the White House in 1789. With the consideration of most governmental representatives having to serve in Washington for an average of four months in the year, the members of Congress took home approximately five hundred dollars a year. Times continued to change, the value of money was, of course, constantly changing, and eventually, in 1816, Congress passed the Compensation Act, according to which their yearly pay increased to one thousand five hundred dollars. After an incredible amount of backlash from the public, and after comprises were made, times progressed steadily up and through what is currently the general pay for a member of Congress, $174,000.

The majority of senators or representatives would be at this pay rate consistently throughout their term, but rates of pay do differ depending on the level of responsibility that the member has, as well. For instance, if a member of the Senate is a majority or minority leader, their earnings may be above $195,000, while the Speaker of the House typically makes about $225,000.

Without considering the additives to these generous salaries, they seem akin to that of most software developers and such. However, there are a fair number of added incentives that those in Congress have the liberty to enjoy, and this is where the built ins for youth representatives would stem from. Apart from the salaries that they reserve, all members of Congress, whether House or Senate, receive allowances to be able to pay staff and cover additional expenses that they may have. On average, a senator's allowance is upwards of three million dollars, while a representative typically enjoys an allowance of over nine hundred thousand dollars. Apart from these expenses, a further three thousand dollars is typically accorded to cover living expenses for time away from their respective localities. Within these plentiful allowances, there is more than enough budget allocations for representatives to include one more member of staff who stand with them to represent their populace at the White House. Balancing the tables to ensure that allowances are meant to incorporate the additional expenses that one representative from each body of Congress of each state would face is a task that the administrators in Washington are far more than qualified for.

An understanding of the representation of youth in governmental positions is incomplete without analyzing the previous efforts that have been put into effect to attempt to create the sought impacts. Throughout history, there have been times when different causes have taken the forefront of social outrage to create disruptions in the day to day functions of the government, thus spurring a need for change. These social issues have ranged from racial bias, to women's rights, to equal employment opportunity, etc., each time attempting to put forward a message to the change makers and lawmakers of the country. Each of these endeavors is backed by a necessity to create change, and while not all movements create overall success, there are several that result in successful change being incorporated into the system.

Although an issue that has been given spurts of importance through debates, literature, and student bodies in the past, social sensationalism has not particularly been able to affect the change makers in regards to the issue of bringing about advocacy for youth representatives. Primarily, this is due to the ingrained ideology that changing the laws of the nation is in the hands of the public to a certain extent, but changing the foundation or structure itself is not. Quite to the contrary, the United States of America was established as a democracy in order to allow for that particular freedom to be available to one and all who are associated with the land. While there are very few ways in which America operates as a true democracy today, the primary reasoning of creating a democracy was to establish a way for the citizenry to create a government that is within their control, rather than being within the clenches of the government, itself. In other words, the famous saying applies, the law is made for people, not the other way around.

Nonetheless, there are brave individuals who have stepped up to the platform to be able to speak out regarding this issue that they perceive as particularly important. The majority of these speakers or promoters of this concept come from educational, scholarly backgrounds, and have taken the study and time to understand human psychology at a deeper level. Amongst these multiple advocates for these concepts, one of the most prominent figures is Pomona College professor John Seery, who authored "Too Young to Run", a read that elaborates upon the ironies of the level of responsibility that citizens are given at the age of majority, and how unfortunate it is, how biased it is, in fact, that running for positions in most official capacities is not amongst those rights.

Seery, like many other advocates in this particular division of the field, elaborates upon the concept of amendments, a built-in adaptability measure in the Constitution. One of the more riveting amendments per the Constitution that references this idea is the twenty-sixth amendment, which clearly outlines the responsibility and ability eighteen year olds have to vote in both state and federal elections. This raises the valid subsequent question, which is that if these individuals are considered responsible enough to choose their next leader, they should be given the opportunity to look at things from the opposite side of the glass.

There are little to no questions surrounding the ability to spark change without causing any legal distress to the congressional bodies. The whole purpose of the inclusion of amendments within the Constitution is to emphasize the idea that society is constantly evolving, and with it, ideals, concepts, ways of life, and, in turn, ways of leading. When creating the Constitution and faced with the dilemma of how to address any and all changes that several centuries of generations would need for the future, the addition of the concept of amendments was to offer forethought on how leadership in the United States may continue after its original leaders.

Would there be an incredible amount of difficulty to add an amendment that is similar enough to the lines of the twenty-sixth in order to ensure that these representatives are given an opportunity? What is the level of change that would be necessitated for this effort to be taken through to success? The answer is quite minimal. It would require an immense amount of support, on top of a very strong basis of contenders who fall under the category of youth leaders, and are ready to take on the severity of tasks that are assigned to them on a daily basis while being able to manage the populace that falls under their leadership.

The historical basis for creating the bar of an age restriction on what age qualifies candidates to stand for different positions of office in the White House is rich with a lot of non-discussion. In essence, there was little to no forethought primarily given to the concept at all, with very few leaders actually standing up to promote otherwise and create discussion around the subject before arriving at a decision. The laughable part of the process, the one most central element that makes it so utterly apparent that the system is due for an update, is that George Mason, a delegate from Virginia, made the decision of the age of eligibility for a position in Congress based on his own life experiences, stating that he was not mature enough to handle duties as large as public consequence at the age of twenty one, further adding that at twenty five, he had felt as though there was a difference, and a maturity of sorts, in his decision making abilities, thus entitling him to be able to run for elected in official positions. Even so, considering that the level of responsibility accorded differs between members of the House and the Senate, as well as further so for other positions in Washington, he created a gap of five year "maturity stops" to allow for the mental and professional growth of individuals aiming to run for office.

During this vast set of decision making discussions, the parties involved almost unanimously agreed that their life experiences led to their assessment of the proposed age restrictions for running for office as fair. One individual, James Wilson of Pennsylvania, stood as the lone objector to this ideology, insisting that putting bars on ages of applicability, in general, would limit the potential that individuals had in expressing their abilities to lead and create a positive spiral of change successfully. He crafted a rather well backed argument, citing that precedent for young leadership had already been set in examples such as former British Prime Minister William Pitt the Younger, who assumed leadership prior to his twenty fifth birthday. As a fantastic leader with an outstanding capacity for creating the results that his people sought, he exemplifies one of several such examples that testify to the capabilities of the youth in leadership capacities.

In spite of the well supported discussions that James Wilson facilitated, the decision to institute the minimum age for applicability to the House of Representatives was set at twenty five through a 7-3 vote. Subsequently, the decision to apply similar age restrictions at thirty for the Senate and thirty five for the presidency were instituted without objection.

These conversations happened at the Constitutional Convention of 1787. In other words, the American public is following a system that was conjured more than two hundred years ago, determining its value addition to the country solely based on the paper value of it being drafted by those who lived in very different times, with very different resources available to them, and a very new establishment within their control. To follow the existing pathway is not a weakness nor a flaw, but rather a pathway for destruction. It is impossible for the American citizenry to conform to all of the initially drafted principles as is with the original Constitution. In fact, the Founding Fathers, and the entirety of the public at the time, was well aware of the need for a capacity of change, thus embedding the ability for there to be amendments made to the Constitution, the coveted document upon which the foundation of the country runs. If there had been no modifications ever made to the document that determines the basis for running the country, there would be no superpower in the place where America stands, there would be no rights for women to attain the level of respect and integrity that they have time and again proven worthy of, and there would no melting pot. The country would have remained stagnant from all directions, and when there is a push for it to keep flowing towards positive bearing change in a multitude of directions, it only makes sense to further those efforts by promoting further positive change.

The arguments made by those who believe that the country is not flawed in presenting a system that is against the growth of youth leadership as representation are simply null and void. They are made upon the basis of time old concepts that have been, for the most part, made passé by the empowerment accorded to sectors of the populace today. Eighty percent of Americans have active smartphone usage, the demographics of which are all over the place, ranging in all arenas, including race, economic status, age, ethnicity, etc., but all singularly fashioned to point out that technology empowers every individual today. Fifty three percent of children own a smartphone before the age of eleven in the present day[18]. Eighty five percent of teenagers between thirteen and eighteen have active smart phone usage in the United States of America[19].

This all points to a clear indicator: the youth of today is far ahead of where the youth in the past generations have been. They are stronger, smarter, more capable, and more knowledgeable than any generation prior has been well before the age of twenty five. When there is a presentation of facts that support that these children have the worldly knowledge and the general capacity to lead, there is no reason other than unseemly monopolization of power by a singular generation to incorporate them into the current ranks of leadership. Furthermore, the children of the present day have been exposed to social issues at such a deep level that they are far more integrated with the daily happenings and the biases present in the world, as well as their anticipated solutions for them, far before their parents have the chance to educate them on these matters. These empowered individuals deserve the chance to prove their capacity to make change happen.

Far too long the United States has hoped for a miracle to make the country the great symbol of power and all things positive that it was once envisioned to represent. That miracle is no further than within the hands of the youth of the nation. That miracle is being intentionally prohibited from being bestowed upon the people. There are innumerable reasons to support why there may be a fear with supplying power to those who are not capable of handling it, but these Millennials and Gen Z representatives are ready to stand up to the same level of scrutiny that any other elected officials would face. They are ready to raise their hands in support of the country they have for so long aimed to see successful. They are spending time pouring their sweat, blood, and tears, so as to say, into becoming the leaders that the society needs, such that they are able to become the change that they wish to see, and stand as examples for all those who came before, and all those that will come after. It is the duty of the American public to stay true to the vow of democracy that the country was built upon, and encourage these members to embody that vision. The results will flow in with the beautiful collaboration of experience and creativity, of time and energy, of maturity and inspiration.

The Constitution was built upon the principles of change because of a mission to break free from the oppressive leaders who governed the pioneers and settlers prior to their arrival to the new land. There were wars fought for the sake of ensuring that no individual would once again feel under the influence or under the power of a body that had the control to cause the public to do their bidding. Two and a half centuries after the wars have been fought, the winnings have been claimed, and the freedom has been earned, the country is finding itself once again at a standstill in this matter. All said and done, a portion of the population that is considered American citizenry, one hundred and twenty seven million people of that group, is still held back from being able to experience that freedom to influence the nation in the ways in which they cumulatively feel there is change to be had. There is no name beyond monopolization of power for the level of non-integrity that the current system of "democracy" in the country truly represents. It's time for that to change. Discord and derailing morals have corrupted the system that was in existence to create an equal society that incorporates a voice for all. The pledge to that star spangled banner as one nation, indivisible, with liberty and justice for all needs to be honored.

The Government's
Spa Day

"If your actions inspire others to dream more, learn more, do more, and become more, you are a leader."

John Quincy Adams proposed this notion of leadership two centuries ago to encourage leaders to take on the roles of mentors, and to encourage their subsequents to do the same. His ideology was and is true, an epitome of how to be an adequate and impressive commander. In today's world of media production that capitalizes upon stories of power being mishandled, misrepresented, or misunderstood, the true capacity for leadership has died down, and those who spoke to it before stand as simply idle memorials to what a leader once was.

A true figure of prominence in society is much more than what their apparent position exemplifies. They stand as role models, with the ability to influence generations to come, and this definition is nowhere truer than it is for those who have the capacity to create change in government. These positions are held by those who truly do intend to be figures respected by all segments of society for their meritorious credentials and abilities, not to mention ideals and actions. These individuals are presented to students at impressionable ages as the ideal member of society to follow the footsteps of. Furthermore, these individuals are marked in history forever as the selected entity to represent the entirety of a group. The selection for those in such positions, then, is a matter of great deliberation and concern if not conducted fairly or in a manner that behooves adequate analysis.

At all three levels of the most effectual elected officials in the White House, direct parts of the public are represented by the decisions that they choose to make during their time in service. A representative who serves in the House of Representatives stands to showcase the entire district or local region that elected them into that capacity of office. Similarly, a member of the Senate who is elected in by the public stands to be recognized as a voice speaking for the entire state from which he/she stands. Overarching responsibilities, indubitably, fall upon the President: the singular member in the White House and the nation who has the ability to influence all decisions, is regarded as the ruler, for all intents and purposes, of the entire country, and is elected in as a voice for the nation in its entirety.

In order to ensure that the right candidates are taken into consideration for such positions in government, then, there is a necessity to be able to judge the eligibility of those in positions of power. The utmost level of importance is assigned to the position of the presidency. For an individual to attain the power of becoming the nation's Commander in Chief, or President, as he/she is more widely known, one must display an extreme amount of sincerity to the country, to the founding principles of the nation, and to the cause of serving the people.

Democracy is a beautiful thing, in that it functions as a manner to be able to judge the level of ambition that a candidate possesses, through the debates, the speeches, and the campaigning, at large, that are all constituent portions of the process of the presidential election. These built in mechanisms to be able to judge the character and principles of an elected official, however, are often misread as acts of entertainment, and are interpreted as so by those who view the entire system as a mockery. Unfortunately, these ideas are the ones that are picked up by the news creation entities, and are therefore propagated as the most recollected incidents from what is initially meant to have served as a keen insight into the candidate themselves.

Regardless, where citizenry is able to wonderfully judge the speaking abilities of a candidate when taking an active interest in the viewership of these campaign based events, it fails in being able to judge the subject matter expertise of that candidate. Article II of the Constitution goes into great detail regarding the responsibilities of the president, as well as the individuals he/she chooses or simply has with them through their term. Throughout Article II, the President of the United States is authorized to power that is to be used in accordance with the checks and balances through the governmental branches, as per the accord of the concept of democracy. Nonetheless, the power that is allocated to the seat of the president is allotted as such with the expectation of the ability to wield it.

Power has always been considered to be an interdependent function of authority and influence, and, as such, the president is to gain his/her power from the level of authority that they assert, by being influential through their possession of knowledge on governance of the nation. In simpler terms, they need to know how to do their job, and how to do it well. When one's job is to lead the country, the pressure in that situation increases exponentially. Accordingly, the accountability increases exponentially, as well. To be quite direct, in previous administrations, although accountability has been high, the knowledge bearing aspect that a leader must possess has absconded, as it may appear.

In a direct analogy, it is easiest to consider positions in alternative fields. Leadership of a country is a sticky area to consider credentials, because it is often true that an individual need not possess the supposedly fancy means to attain knowledge prior to their acceptance of their term, given that they do have a passion for the governance that they are being assigned to, as well as a passion towards the betterment of the people who are under their charge during their term. In essence, a lack of knowledge is not intended to be an allowance for individuals to take on roles as challenging as the presidency; rather, it is to be substituted by the presence of factors such as zeal, which are human interests that go above and beyond the simplicity of book bearing knowledge that is acquirable.

As a matter of fact, taking on the role of a presidency or representative for a state in some capacity, is a burden rather than a gift if that individual does not already possess the aforementioned ardor for their position and the consequent functions. An approximate thirty three percent of Americans believe that the leadership in place is incompetent not because of their inability to perform in the capacity for which they have been elected, but rather their non-willingness to actually incorporate the consistent vehemence to make each day another opportunity to improve the society that they serve.

The more power that one acquires, the more responsibility that they amenably acquire, as well. As a tried and true statement, it is evident that there are few positions that truly stand for this over and above the presidency. The President of the United States deserves to be tested thoroughly prior to taking office. In fact, prior to rising to candidacy, this individual should prove themselves as dedicated to the cause, by investing the time necessary to acquire the knowledge that is required to run the nation. When any institution reviews an individual's eligibility to take on a role, the first and foremost observances made surround the ability of that individual to either already possess or be able to possess the knowledge required to perform the capacities of that position well. In political areas, the knowledge required is best exhibited through a mastery of the foundational concepts of the country. This goes above and beyond the means of a high school classroom, but the very fundamental ideas that are present even at that scale need to be revisited for a large majority of the candidates who present themselves as potential leaders in the present political climate of the United States of America.

To break down each of the fundamental structures that act as pillars to hold together the system of democracy that the country has adapted, one need look no further than the documents upon which each citizen is encouraged to review their rights and duties towards their country. These documents are marks of the construction of the country, similar to blueprints of a house, and any engineer making improvements to a structure, or any politician making process changes to the law of the country, should have an active understanding of such blueprints.

Among the vast multitude of the documents that are necessary in the process of understanding the nation's foundation, the Constitution itself is the most critical.

The Constitution is composed of multiple elements:

- The Preamble that introduces the document, along with the purpose of its creation and the conditions of its integration into the Founding Documents

- The Body that contains the first three articles of the document, each dedicated to describing an independent branch of the government. The three branches of the United States government are the Legislative, Judicial, and Executive branches, of which the responsibilities and privileges of each are described within these three articles. In addition, the body contains articles four through seven, which are all cumulatively meant to describe the relationships between the aforementioned branches of government, and how to maintain compliance with the original vision of the Constitution through any and all changes that may be added to it over time.

- Several amendments that describe the ways in which the Constitution has been altered to support the adaptations of the country to the conditions of the present day society. The first ten of these amendments have been pulled together to be collectively referred to as the Bill of Rights.

This individual document holds the answers to a majority of the questions posed regarding duties, responsibilities, rights, and abilities for the citizenry of the United States. However, it also serves as a basis for the entirety of the nation to assess the effectuality of the governmental entities in place. It provides keen insight into the original vision that the founders of the country had put into deciding what America is meant to be, how to assist it on its path to the pinnacle of success that it continues to strive for. Further, it provides the factors of decision making for citizens to determine what a responsible leader would truly resemble in the face of the nation's many qualifiable candidates. Those who would abuse rather than use power can be swiftly identified through their observable qualities, and those who have an understanding of the power that they hope to wield can be separated from the pack of candidates by assessing their hold on understanding this, amongst other, documents.

The only way to truly ensure that the president, or other elected officials, of the nation are capable of employing the power of the seat they wish to claim is to test them on their knowledge of the country's political climate, as well as their capacity to successfully lead. Each candidate, regardless of party affiliation, previous experience, educational credentials, etc., must be subject to an examination administered by the Government of the United States, which tests the individual's understanding of the nation's founding documents, including the Constitution, the Declaration of Independence, the Federalist Papers, as well as past and present treaties, agreements, and political affiliations of the United States.

As an all rounding assessment of a candidate for an elected office should be, these assessments would be expected to cater to the level of specialty that would apply to each respective area of public service. For those serving in purely local capacities, their knowledge base should be extensive enough to cover any and all material that describes their entity's political nature, inclusive of the demographics, current political issues, areas for improvement, active efforts and committees, as well as past initiatives and financial standings. Similarly, for those on state or national levels, their examinations would be comprehensively covering the respective areas at greater depths, with the complexity of each exam increasing with impact on legislature, most likely posing subsequently greater levels of difficulty for governors, representatives, and senators. With no doubt, the most detailed level of analysis would occur with the president, and as such, their competence should be scrutinized the most.

In general, the qualifications that are expected for a presidential candidate range from passion, to background, to, strangely enough, popularity. However, none of these qualifications tend to pose questions regarding the most necessary qualities of a leader, namely the abilities to display intellect, a propensity for leadership, and the ability to speak fluently in American politics and history. In the plethora of observable characteristics that a hopeful candidate may portray, these three direct the majority of the events and responsibilities that they actually undertake during their time serving in their position. In most senses, it is unfathomable to have the entire country's leadership under a candidate who may or may not have the abilities necessary to continue a several year long term successfully, resulting in positive diplomacy and financially sound decisions.

To this means, a test designed for the presidency should be inclusive of a large number of subject areas, including the following:

1. **American History (10%)**
   - This is an absolutely pertinent area of knowledge for a presidential candidate, because the reasoning behind most previous political decisions, and the key takeaways from previous administrations is hidden within these subject areas. Although a president will always have a very knowledgeable staff to support them and provide more insight into their decisions

before they are made, it is sensible that a president should be sound in their decision making abilities independent of these advisors, and having a very solid understanding of what has and what has not been in the favor of the country from past political endeavors is a key mechanism to making it happen.

2. **Political Diplomacy (10%)**

- Right down to student level, those who are interested in political science fields have a very large background in diplomacy, and are often seen partaking in events and networking arenas where their abilities to perform their diplomatic speaking skills are present. For a president, it is not enough to be able to speak in a way that calls for action or that speaks to connect to the public. This is the most common type of speech that is observed through campaigning, and while it is the optimal type of speech that would serve a candidate through their campaigning season, after taking office, they are required to demonstrate an exorbitant amount of diplomacy to successfully create longstanding good relationships, nationally and internationally.

3. **Global Current Events (5%)**

- Especially in the United States, national leaders have a very large hand in international affairs, and should have a very good handle on what the state of global current events is in order to gauge the level of support that is reasonable for exterior conflicts, along with what is feasible and driven politically correctly for the image of the country on an international platform. The leader of each country, especially one that is as revered as the United States of America, plays a key role in international forums such as the United Nations, whereby it would not behoove a candidate to be unaware of what current political states are internationally.

4. **National Crises and Initiatives (25%)**

- By and far the most important portion of the test for a national leader, the president should be able to showcase a very prominent ability to assess and address national crises. He/She should also have the drive and ability to put forward concepts for initiatives on how to address those crises as a solution provider, so as to provide a level of confidence to the public in the ability of a leader to partake in resolutions of conflicts in all stages. Often times, this assesses the emotional quotient and political diplomacy of a leader all in one, because a president is expected to have the decorum to present a statement, especially on tragic events, that is empathetic, but measured enough to assure the society that such risks are being mitigated through active initiatives to resolve the base issue behind the event.

Furthermore, the test must include questions surrounding the demographics and economic situations of multiple areas of the United States. This will serve as an indicator of the candidate's ability to connect with those he/she desires to serve, and will show their knowledge about their potential constituents. Demographics are highly separated throughout the country, and generally very spread out across regions, in spite of statistics being misleading about particular regions. As a result, a presidential candidate should make it their priority to know how to address issues such as economic poverty conditions on an overarching national basis, but also on an individualized local basis, because the solutions for issues relating to economics, especially, can never be one size fits all.

5. Economic Assessment (10%)

- As always, a candidate being presented for a position of national governance holds the responsibility of also being able to understand the conditions of all those under them who happen to fall under their wing for leadership. The grander the scale of the position, the larger the set of associated responsibility, and the candidate's ability to gauge that is easily tested through their economic assessment of multiple areas across the country. Of course, research and advisors are necessary to gain the most granular levels of details surrounding economic conditions in an area, but it is easily understood that a candidate should have invested time to learn about their people, and the country that they plan to lead prior to making an application towards actually assuming that position. This level of testing will be an accurate provider to learn just how much effort a candidate has invested into learning about their country and their constituents.

On a basis of understanding the present day conditions of the government and the country, these areas of questioning are primarily prefatory. The next level of investment of time that would be expected from a candidate who plans to run for political office would be an understanding of the documentation that runs the nation itself. At the level of the presidential candidacy, this would be based off of quite a large set of documents.

6. Constitutional Literacy (10%)

- It is unfair to expect every political candidate to come in with a political science background. In fact, it would be quite unethical to pose such a requirement, because of the acceptance of the large variety of backgrounds that a candidate could come from to actually assume the position of a very capable leader. However, it is essential for a leader to be knowledgeable at lengths over and above the general public regarding the governance measures of the country. This portion of the exam would be a multifaceted question set, posing mostly multiple choice questions on the Constitution, the Declaration of Independence, the Federalist Papers, and existing and past treaties, agreements, committees, etc. Primarily, this portion will serve to showcase the potential candidate's ability to speak intelligently and politically literately on the subjects that guide their daily interactions with other members of government, whether national or international. Especially in recent times, it has been seen that even small political misspeaking can reveal a much larger flaw in the ability of an individual to serve as president, and can cause massive areas of concern. Who would employ a lawyer who is unfamiliar with the proceedings of a court? Who would hire a doctor who is unfamiliar with using a stethoscope? Similarly, who would elect a leader who is illiterate politically?

The examination would not, of course, be complete without questions that judge the candidate's ability in general leadership, including negotiations, styles of leadership, decision making, organizational structure, etc. Although it may seem counterintuitive, the American populace needs more than just a leader of the people. The individual in power must also be a leader of the nation, and these skills are absolutely necessary for the person taking office in these capacities to possess.

7. Logical Decision Making (10%)

- It goes without saying that the best type of leader is one who makes logical decisions that have strong foundations in reasoning, and are primarily inarguably favorable for the American public. As such, there should be an assessment of how effectively a candidate can even make logical decisions on smaller levels, such as being able to see patterns, analyze differences, and provide coherent responses to questions that challenge logic. Every political science position that does require an examination, namely legal ones, do have a heavy influence in logic. For instance, law school admissions tests are the most steeply logical tests that are available for students to undertake. There reasoning behind this sort of construction of a test is that someone in the capacity to make decisions and arguments for another party should be highly logical, and be able to make keen observations that may not otherwise be visible. This is not to be confused with general intelligence, or IQ. These two standards are vastly different, primarily because IQ challenges speed, visual interpretation, and a large number of other areas that tap into the entire brain to assess its effectiveness in multiple particular categories. In this portion of the exam, the only aim is to be able to gain an understanding of the decision making style of the candidate, and a judgment of impulse levels in that candidate.

8. Emotional Intelligence (10%)

- Beyond being logical, a candidate should have an immense amount of control over their EQ (emotional quotient) in order to be an effective leader. This metric measures the ability of an individual to display the several characteristics that are typical of leadership capacities, including the ability to react appropriately and calmly to situations, the ability to reign in emotions and act as an influencer and resolver in capacities that require it, and to have a good handle over assessing people, as well as their particular qualities. A candidate who struggles with maintaining EQ will be ineffective in spite of having other political prowess, because they will be unable to withstand the level of pressure that inevitably come with large and very visible positions. Similarly, it is pertinent to note that a leader in a capacity such as the presidency is a highly visible character, and is representative of the entire country. That representative should be well balanced, and considered as an example or role model of who to be, rather than a mockery or an easy meme.

9. Leadership Abilities (10%)

- Ironically obvious, a leader should be well aware of how to lead. For all intents and purposes, there are levels of specific education behind leadership that would be unnecessary to undertake the position of performing leadership rather than studying it, but there should be an inbuilt ability to lead for any leader running for national or international level positions. It is laughable to assume that a leader would be an ineffective one simply because their capacity for being a figure of authority was not assessed before their assumption of the position, but it is an unfortunate event that has occurred plentifully throughout American history. Styles of leadership and abilities to lead can best be observed through personality assessments. For all intents and purposes, the ability to lead is part of the personality of an individual, and their propensity to undertake leadership capacities will also be highly connected to the type of personality that they inherently display.

Voters will be far more well informed if they are equipped with the information given from this test to decide upon a leader. It may be perceived as a bold move to suggest the use of an individual test on one singular day to assess the capacity an individual has for leadership, and there may be multiple particularities that need to be worked out to factor in the daily surprises of life, but a leader of a nation does not have the privilege of having ease during their period of leadership. The President of the United States is under the constant pressure of being the sole decision maker for three hundred and twenty eight million people, and the weight of that burden is almost as heavy as the joy of its rewarding nature when a decision made works wonderfully in their favor. A leader is meant to be prepared for any and all circumstances, and while an exam on paper will never be comprehensive enough to judge their real life experiences or abilities, it is an excellent starting point to be able to judge the capacity that an individual truly has to be a leader.

First and foremost, these scores should be highly visible to the public. While the exam taking process should be very private and conducted by an unbiased panel, the results should be released to the entirety of the public, with specifics of the score breakdowns being provided so that the American people achieve a comprehensive understanding of the individual that they are learning about, which they can then pair with the other qualities they see through that individual's campaigning to decide who their vote goes to.

The scores from these examinations should be taken into consideration when choosing which candidates are capable of proceeding to the level of officially being considered as contenders for the position of the presidency. In fact, scores on this exam should be used as a benchmark standard to decide who should be awarded the honor of being a candidate for the presidential election, the boundaries of which would be set by the Government of the United States. Similar to how votes are counted and collected in full presence of the appropriate governmental authorities by the current President of the United States, the scores should be calculated, and the candidacy eligibility decided upon, in full presence of unbiased figures, as well. The principle of democracy would not allow for there to be any sort of bias surrounding the educational requirements necessary to serve as the president of the nation. Indeed, it would be inappropriate to mandate these, as well, seeing as experience and ability come in numerous forms, none of which are limited to the credentials or the resume that the candidate possesses. Conducting an examination of a potential candidate, however, helps in showing the realism and the ability of the candidate to take responsibility of their position, should they be elected.

In the present day, there are a multitude of issues surrounding the president's inability to interpret and follow the Constitution appropriately, thus requiring the emphasis on the founding documents within any benchmark assessment. This comes from inexperience in the field, perhaps, but more so from a lack of personal motivation to lead the nation and the people. When there is motivation to do one or the other, but not both, there is a leader present, but not a leader of a nation. Certainly not a leader who has the capacity to endanger populaces and integrate changes in the foundation of the nation. In a case example, for instance, one can take the recent issue of birthright citizenship. Although this has been considered, and, indeed, moved away from the spotlight since, reflection upon the occurrences during the time of debate surrounding it are key indicators of what danger the lack of examination of a leader's knowledge can create.

In this instance, the leaders responsible for the interpretation and the protection of the people's rights, as per the Constitution, were unaware of their responsibilities and duties. In specific, the Constitution's Fourteenth Amendment, which was the cause for the debate, was read, but not understood by those in power.

"All persons born or naturalized in the United States and subject to the jurisdiction thereof, are citizens of the United States and of the State wherein they reside. No State shall make or enforce any law which shall abridge the privileges or immunities of citizens of the United States; nor shall any State deprive any person of life, liberty, or property, without due process of law; nor deny to any person within its jurisdiction the equal protection of the laws."

There are a plethora of potential political interpretations of this statement, as well as mannerisms in which to take action when it is called into question as an unclear statement. However, a leader in this position is expected to have the knowledge basis to be able to recall and accurately assess that statement, since it is a portion of the foundational documents of the United States. For a leader to recite irrelevant statements from other documents as a comparison basis, or to lose their emotional quotient when put under the spotlight for not having the correct understanding of the statement is a measure of their ability to lead, or lack thereof. Politically speaking, the mannerisms that are characteristic of a leader empower them to channelize debates and conversations that may explore the multitude of perspectives, since this matter is so specifically concerning the rights of the people under governance. Similarly, the diplomacy of a candidate would be so utterly obvious in this position, since it lends itself, like any debate, to conflicting perspectives and opinions that may create uncomfortable situations for those possessing one side of the viewpoint or another.

Regardless of the political outcome, the American citizenry would do well to assess the abilities of a leader before they elect them to their position, in an act of proaction, rather than reaction. Without a doubt, the statistics of satisfied citizenry will yield more pleasant numbers, with an upwards trend, seeing as individuals would be more aware of who they chose prior to their taking office.

Inevitably, there are mannerisms that adapt as individuals grow, and the same is true for any leader. After assuming office, there are ways in which they can grow, learn, adapt, and shape their ideas which primarily guide their day to day decision making. Nevertheless, having a very keen interpretive understanding of what they positioned their perspectives at prior to taking office will allow for a much more committed analysis of how they have evolved after taking on their role. Overall, this will create a more commutative environment in the White House and beyond, and will overall result in a community that is more enriching for all.

Are you ready to run for President? Take the quiz below and find out how well you score!

Please note: this assessment is purely for entertainment and should not be confused to be an official assessment of any sort. Regardless, it serves as a fantastic template of what one might see a future assessment for the presidency resemble.

American History (5 questions)

1. Which of the following has never served as the capital city?

A. Philadelphia, Pennsylvania

B. Annapolis, Maryland

C. Princeton, New Jersey

D. Chicago, Illinois

2. What year did the American Civil War end?

A. 1776

B. 1820

C. 1865

D. 1994

3. What was the deadliest battle in American history?

A. The Battle of Antietam

B. The storming of Normandy

C. The Battle at Valley Forge

D. The Boston Tea Party

4. When did the Revolutionary War end?

A. 1776

B. 1783

C. 1882

D. 1720

5. Who was the first President of the United States?

   A. Peyton Randolph

   B. George Washington

   C. Thomas Mifflin

   D. John Hancock

Political Diplomacy (5 questions)

6. Which of the following is not an international organization?

   A. World Court

   B. United Nations

   C. Organization of American States

   D. International Money Fund

7. What is the full form of NATO?

   A. North Atlantic Tourism Organization

   B. North American Treaty Organization

   C. North Atlantic Treaty Organization

D. New American Treaty Operations

8. Where is the headquarters for NATO?

   A. Brussels, Belgium

   B. Paris, France

   C. Washington, D.C.

   D. London, United Kingdom

9. Which of the following is a developing country?

   A. The United States of America

   B. Pakistan

   C. The United Kingdom

   D. Australia

10. Who is the current leader of the United Nations?

   A. Ban ki-Moon

   B. António Guterres

   C. Donald Trump

   D. Narendra Modi

Global Current Events (2 questions)

11. Where did the novel coronavirus originate?

A. Tokyo, Japan

B. Wuhan, China

C. Mumbai, India

D. Philadelphia, Pennsylvania, USA

12. What is the Israeli-Palestinian conflict about?

A. Territory ownership

B. Women's rights

C. Monarchy

D. Slavery

National Crises (5 questions)

13. What is the poverty rate in the United States today?

A. 25.4%

B. 11.8%

C. 4.5%

D. 54.6%

14. Which of the following is not considered a national issue?

    A. Unemployment rates

    B. Poverty

    C. COVID-19

    D. Education rights

15. What percentage of global energy consumption is from the United States?

    A. Under 5 percent

    B. Between 5 and 10 percent

    C. Between 10 and 15 percent

    D. Above 15 percent

16. Which of the following is not a current public national concern?

A. Gun rights

B. Abortion

C. Drug use

D. Agricultural methods

17. What is the most polluted city in the country?

    A. New York, New York

    B. Fairbanks, Alaska

    C. Washington, D.C.

    D. Chicago, Illinois

Economic Assessment (5 questions)

18. The largest percentage of personal income for Americans comes from:

    A. Landlord rent

    B. Tax reimbursements

    C. Wages and salaries

    D. Interest from stocks and bonds

19. Who would benefit if the United States stopped any imports of cars from Germany?

    A. Car manufacturers in the United States

    B. Consumers in the United States

    C. Car manufacturers in Germany

    D. Production facilities in China

20. Resources available are limited for use, so Americans should:

    A. Reduce their usage
    B. Be mindful about usage
    C.   Obtain additional resources
    D. Disregard availability

21. When governments supply products or services, who generally benefits from these?

    A. Small businesses
    B. Those who pay for the respective products and services
    C. All homeless individuals
    D. Several individuals, regardless of paying

22. When the federal government's expenditures are greater than revenue for a year, that difference is referred to as:

    A. National debt
    B. Budget surplus

C. Budget deficit

D. Economic fallout

Constitutional Literacy (5 questions)

23. How were the deputies to the Constitutional Convention chosen?

    A. They were randomly selected from a lottery style

    B. They were appointed by the States

    C. They were elected

    D. They were chosen from the Revolutionary War

24. What is the second amendment in the Bill of Rights?

    A. Freedom of religion

    B. Freedom of due process

    C. Freedom of speech

    D. Freedom to vote

25. Who is the "Father of the Constitution"?

    A. William Penn

    B. Thomas Jefferson

C. James Madison

D. George Washington

26. Who presented the Virginia Plan?

A. Edmund Randolph

B. William Randolph

C. George Washington

D. James Madison

27. What are the parts of the Constitution?

A. The Introduction, Body, and Conclusion

B. The Preamble, Body, and Conclusion

C. The Preamble, Body, and Amendments

D. The Body, Amendments, and Conclusion

Logical Decision Making (2 questions)

28. What is a benefit of reframing?

A. Large production jumps

B. Prevention of harassment

C. Generation of new ideas

D. Lowering losses

29. Determining feasibility, while assessing costs and benefits, is which part of the decision making process?

   A. Contemplating alternatives

   B. Identifying alternatives

   C. Collecting relevant information

   D. Weighing alternatives

Emotional Intelligence (2 questions)

30. One of the key factors of emotional intelligence is:

   A. Self-management

   B. Self-awareness

   C. Social awareness

   D. All of the above

31. A contributor with a positive attitude and good performance is likely to achieve each of the following except for:

   A. Being appreciated by coworkers

B. Jealousy from coworkers

C. Favorable work conditions

D. Higher productivity

Leadership Abilities (2 questions)

32. All of the following are traits of effective leaders except:

A. Trustworthiness and strong character

B. Openness and transparency

C. Highly motivated

D. Confidence to achieve all goals independently

33. The Pygmalion effect shows that:

A. Setting high expectations elevates performance

B. Setting low expectations creates comfortable work environments

C. Setting low expectations will frustrate workers

D. Setting high expectations will frustrate workers

How did you do?

American History (5 questions)

D, C, A, B, A

Political Diplomacy (5 questions)

C, C, A, B, B

Global Current Events (2 questions)

B, A

National Crises (5 questions)

B, D, D, D, B

Economic Assessment (5 questions)

C, A, B, D, C

Constitutional Literacy (5 questions)

B, C, C, A, C

Logical Decision Making (2 questions)

C, D

Emotional Intelligence (2 questions)

D, B

Leadership Abilities (2 questions)

D, A

References

1. Pew Research Center, 2017

2. Pew Research Center, 2017

3. CQ Press, 2018

4. Gallup, 2020

5. Pew Research Center, 2017

6. American Progress, 2018

7. Pew Research Center, 2018

8. United States Senate, 2018

9. U.S. Bureau of Labor Statistics, American Time Use Survey, 2020

10. Pew Research Center, 2018

11. Pew Research Center, 2018

12. Pew Research Center, 2017

13. Pew Research Center, 2018

14. Pew Research Center, 2017

15. McKinsey & Company, 2019

16. McKinsey & Company, 2019

17. Pew Research Center, 2018

18. Gallup, 2020

19. Gallup, 2020

Critical Review by Dr. Suraj Malhan

The Purple Wave offers thought provoking ideas regarding the voter-ship of the United States, as well as its political future. Throughout the writing, there are mentions regarding the ability of the citizenry to match up to the expectations that had been set through the formation of the Constitution, and, accordingly, delegated duties to the public. It further goes into an analysis of the ways in which leaders are selected and the manners in which a governing body is decided upon.

Ashraya shines light on many of the subjects that are today considered controversial and hushed, as well as those that are perhaps left in the dark because of the monopolization of power that has become the norm of the day in political climates throughout the nation. Amongst the multitude of points that she makes, one consistently asserted viewpoint is that the youth have more duty towards the nation than afore implemented. With the level of accorded individuality and knowledge bearing capacity that has become a privilege for members of upcoming generations today, there comes a significant turn of responsibility, as well. Perhaps this point requires deeper analysis, though.

Ashraya mentions points of evidence for supporting the perspective that the youth of today are well equipped, educationally and exposure wise, to lead side by side with their more experienced counterparts. One unexplored area, though, is the emotional quotient of the youth of today, and, therefore, the one component of leadership that was left unnoticed when imploring newer generations to acquire prominence.

Of course, one arena where she ensures this point is not amiss is in the requirement of testing for future leaders. In her comprehensive concept of an assessment, she incorporates a decent amount of exposure to the concept of emotional intelligence, and, consequently, ability to lead with the emotional maturity that is the other feared misstep for most youth political leaders. Regardless, this particular point requires individual research to determine the propensity of leadership for those who aim to take responsibility in the capacity of leadership at any and all levels, especially regarding governmental roles, as she suggests.

The Purple Wave touches on concepts that are existent in society, but subdued, because of their inciting nature of political misgivings. In one coherent thought, it serves as the "guide to built a youth-centric future", and gives readers a brilliant overview of what the system is currently producing in the form of objective and subjective results, as well as what the ideal changes made would be. Ashraya goes far into the depths of the nature of politics, which is muddled in its current state of affairs, as she describes. While it is not without debatability, it is fruitful in its provision of a thought process that will stimulate voters to perhaps consider evolving their current conductions. It has a driven purpose as a catalyst for change that was amiss in prior adaptations to the system.

Overall, it creates an omniscience of a brighter tomorrow.

Suraj J. Malhan, DO, MS

Dr. Suraj Malhan graduated with honors from the Philadelphia College of Osteopathic Medicine and will be completing his residency in Neurology at the University of Maryland Medical Center in Baltimore, MD. While juggling the rigors of residency, he continues to be energetically involved with healthcare activism and grassroots advocacy campaigns. He advocates for patients on social, economic, and educational platforms, and encourages policy reform at local, state, and federal levels. His leadership in national organizations and active political involvement led to his induction into the Omega Beta Iota: National Osteopathic Political Honor Society. He was further inducted into the Gold Humanism Honor Society for his compassion towards patients, excellence in clinical care, and devotion to community service.

About the Author

Ashraya Ananthanarayanan

Ashraya is a legal studies graduate of Harvard University, and is currently pursuing further studies at the University of Pennsylvania and the University of London. She holds positions as a Vice President and Chief of Staff in executive operations capacities at technological firms, as well. Ashraya has a passion for political science and social development, and is the recipient of the President's Call to Service Award, Daily Point of Light Award, and PETA's Most Compassionate Award, among several others. Furthermore, she has received accolades from Governors and Senators for her social improvement efforts and her ardent mission to advance the level of involvement of the youth in their communities. *The Purple Wave* is her fourth published book, and her enthusiastic initiative for creating a ripple effect of positive political involvement from the upcoming generations.

www.ingramcontent.com/pod-product-compliance
Lightning Source LLC
Chambersburg PA
CBHW070808240726
48654CB00007B/256